Brief Notes

MAINTENANCE

The publications in *Brief Notes* are outlines of core topics of interest to professionals involved in shopping center management. The outlines are capsule overviews of each topic. Many key points are covered, and shopping center examples are provided for further illustration. Core concepts in each area guide you on topics you may want to explore further. Each outline also contains a helpful glossary.

Brief Notes is designed to provide a helpful and informative overview of the topics covered. It is not intended to be a substitute for more extensive learning that can be achieved through attending ICSC educational programs and reading additional ICSC professional publications.

The outlines contained in *Brief Notes: Shopping Center Management:*

- Management Overview
- Finance
- Insurance and Risk Management
- The Lease and Its Language
- Leasing Strategies
- Maintenance
- Marketing
- Retailing
- Security

Brief Notes

MAINTENANCE

International Council of Shopping Centers
New York

ABOUT THE INTERNATIONAL COUNCIL OF SHOPPING CENTERS

The International Council of Shopping Centers (ICSC) is the trade association of the shopping center industry. Serving the shopping center industry since 1957, ICSC is a not-for-profit organization with over 44,000 members in 77 countries worldwide.

ICSC members include shopping center

- owners
- developers
- managers
- marketing specialists
- leasing agents
- retailers
- researchers
- attorneys

- architects
- contractors
- consultants
- investors
- lenders and brokers
- academics
- public officials

ICSC sponsors more than 200 meetings a year and provides a wide array of services and products for shopping center professionals, including deal making events, conferences, educational programs, accreditation, awards, publications and research data.

For more information about ICSC, write or call the
International Council of Shopping Centers
1221 Avenue of the Americas
New York, NY 10020-1099
Telephone: 646-728-3800
Fax: 212-589-5555
info@icsc.org
http://www.icsc.org

This publication is designed to provide accurate and authoritative information in regard to the subject matter covered. It is sold with the understanding that the publisher is not engaged in rendering legal, accounting, or other professional services. If legal advice or other expert assistance is required, the services of a competent professional person should be sought.

> —*From a Declaration of Principles jointly adopted by a Committee of the American Bar Association and a Committee of Publishers.*

Companies, professional groups, clubs and other organizations may qualify for special terms when ordering quantities of more than 20 of this title.

Published by
International Council of Shopping Centers
Publications Department
1221 Avenue of the Americas
New York, NY 10020-1099

ICSC Catalog No.: 242

ISBN: 1-58268-028-0

Contents

Preface

S hopping center maintenance involves the upkeep of roofs, parking lots, landscaping, electrical equipment, mechanical systems, floors, vertical surfaces, plumbing, and all other common areas shared by all tenants of the center. Usually it is the responsibility of the landlord or the center manager to coordinate center maintenance with tenants. Parameters for this relationship are spelled out in the lease document. Responsibilities for each party (standard operating procedures) are often written down in manual form.

Proper maintenance is crucial to a shopping center because it (1) creates a pleasing and inviting environment for the shopper, (2) bolsters the tenant/landlord relationship, (3) lessens liability risk and (4) leads to energy efficiency. All these factors prolong the economic life of a property and enhance the net operating income for the landlord.

Maintenance will be one of the major expenses incurred by both landlord and tenant in a shopping center. Proper maintenance management can help ease this financial burden.

Although shopping center maintenance covers a wide variety of esoteric topics and procedures, becoming a better maintenance manager need not be a difficult task. This book details key points that will help you—the shopping center professional—better understand basic maintenance and outlines practices that will improve management skills.

Acknowledgments

The material in this outline is based in part on a course presented at the International Council of Shopping Centers (ICSC) John T. Riordan School for Professional Development Management Institute.

The International Council of Shopping Centers gratefully acknowledges the individuals mentioned below, who have contributed their expertise to this publication.

Phil Carlson, SCSM, Vice President, Property Management, The Macerich Company
Stephen J. Coates, CSM, CCIM, CPM, Coates & Sowards, Inc.
Barbara J. English, Shopping Center Consultant
N. Gary Sowards, CPM, Vice President, Coates & Sowards, Inc.

Core Concepts

✓ Upkeep, repair and replacement of physical plant

✓ Exterior/shell: roof, parking, landscaping, snow removal

✓ Interior: floors, glass, walls, ceilings

✓ Mechanical/electrical: HVAC, vertical transportation, electrical

SHOPPING CENTER MAINTENANCE

Shopping center maintenance is the preservation and enhancement of a shopping center through the upkeep, repair and replacement of the physical plant and mechanical systems.

The lease document establishes maintenance responsibility between tenant and landlord.

Typically, the tenant is responsible for maintenance of leased space and the landlord for all common areas (unleased space shared by all tenants) and shared systems within the center. For example, the cleaning of carpet within a store space will be performed by the tenant. The cleaning of a tile floor immediately outside the store in the common area of the center will be the responsibility of the landlord.

The products and systems most likely to be the responsibility of the landlord in a standard lease document are:

- Roof
- Parking lot, other asphalt areas, sidewalks, curbs, and gutters
- Landscaping/irrigation systems
- Heating, ventilation and air conditioning (HVAC), other electrical systems that serve the common area, and energy management systems
- Lighting (in the common area)
- Floors (in the common area)
- Utilities (in the common area)
- Sprinklers and riser rooms
- Alarm and P.A. systems
- Plumbing
- Door and locks
- Vertical transportation (elevators and escalators)

In addition, a landlord is likely to be responsible for the following services:

- Security
- Trash removal
- Snow removal
- Sweeping of parking lots
- Main mall signage
- Insurance for the structure and common area
- Property taxes billed back to tenant unless separately assessed for tenant

- Management fee (services performed by a management company on behalf of the landlord for the benefit of the tenant). The fee is usually a percentage of the center's gross monthly receipts.

Core Concepts

✓ Inspections and scheduling
✓ Preventive maintenance
✓ Documentation
✓ Budgeting

THE MAINTENANCE PROCESS

The following steps generally constitute the maintenance process:

- Communication with tenant: The establishment of a working relationship between the center owner and tenants to better maintain shared assets
- Scheduling of inspection and maintenance: The time and place when inspection and maintenance procedures will be performed, including scheduled preventive maintenance.
- Property inspection: A detailed examination of the physical assets of a shopping center that determines what, if any, maintenance, repair or replacement work needs to be done

- Maintenance work: The basic work needed to keep an asset in efficient operating condition
- Equipment replacement: The substitution of new equipment for old when life expectancy is reached and it becomes economically advantageous to replace equipment
- Documentation: A thorough record keeping of all upkeep, repair and replacement work done on a shopping center
- Budget: Simply stated, the computation of how much it costs to maintain a shopping center. The budget is often tabulated on a yearly and per-project cost basis. For example, an emergency repair requires a revision of the budget and separate cost analysis.

Core Concepts

✓ Aesthetics
✓ Safety
✓ Efficiency in energy management

GOALS OF A MAINTENANCE PROGRAM

A well-maintained center will have a positive effect on sales, often resulting in favorable rental rates and increased leasing interest. It will also help create favorable consumer perception, satisfied tenants, and better bottom-line performance.

The aims of a well-run maintenance program include:

- Aesthetic appeal: A well-maintained, good-looking center will entice the consumer, improve relations with tenants and your community and aid in leasing and increasing sales
- Safety and security: Constant maintenance helps eliminate potential liabilities
- Energy conservation: Continual inspection of mechanical

equipment ensures a cost-saving operation. Also, regular inspection offers an owner the opportunity to replace obsolete equipment with a more energy-efficient product. For example, fluorescent tubes in the common area can be replaced with newer, energy-saving units.

■ Avoidance of crisis management: A maintenance program provides an accurate picture of a center for a landlord. Unexpected, expensive-to-fix failures are less likely to happen.

■ Developing relationships: Maintenance can establish and strengthen the bond between landlord, tenant, and local community.

■ Preventive maintenance: A program to extend the life and efficiencies of systems.

■ Competitive edge: A well-maintained center can give you a competitive edge in your marketplace.

Core Concepts

✓ Landlord responsibilities
  under the lease
✓ CAM recoveries
✓ Standard Operating
  Procedures

MAINTENANCE GUIDELINES

The lease, the signed agreement between landlord and tenant, provides the guidelines for the manager. It is important for the following reasons:

- Establishes responsibility: The lease document clearly outlines the maintenance responsibilities of the landlord and the tenant. It defines what is common area and the duty of the landlord to maintain and what is leased space and maintained by the tenant.
- Sets standards: The lease describes maintenance to be performed, according to standards set by the landlord. These criteria may be outlined and explained formally as in the *Standard Operating Procedures Manual* (see below), or

briefly summarized in lease language obligations of the landlord such as the following:

> Landlord or its agents shall operate, repair, equip and maintain the Common Area in a manner deemed by Landlord in its business judgment to be reasonable and appropriate and consistent with other shopping centers located in the same state.

Landlords and managers must also be familiar with safety and other standards set by city, state and federal governments. These standards will have an effect on how a property is maintained. For example, certain municipalities will not allow a replacement roof to be placed over an existing roof. The tear-off of the existing roof will add cost to any roof-replacement procedure. The landlord should make the tenant aware of this possibility.

- States what is recoverable from the tenant: The lease establishes CAM (common area maintenance) for each tenant. In addition, the document will outline which capital expenses are also the responsbility of the occupant. For example, tenants pay for maintenance and repair of the parking lots through CAM. The construction of a new parking deck to expand parking capabilities would be a structural expense paid by the landlord.

All leases are not the same, and this will have an effect on maintenance procedures. For example, maintenance fees on a triple net lease (in which the tenant pays 100 percent of the taxes, insurance and maintenance involved with operating in a center) will be different from charges associated with a gross lease (in which the landlord pays all of the taxes, insurance and maintenance of a shopping center). In addition, anchor tenants will often insist on using their own leases, with provisions not included in the standard lease for the smaller tenants of a shopping center.

Standard operating procedures are a course of action stating precisely how a particular system or policy is to be conducted. They are usually set down in the center's *Standard Operating Procedures Manual*, which informs the manager and center staff how, where and when maintenance is to be performed on equipment and real property. Standard operating procedures will vary greatly from center to center, depending upon variables such as location, weather, state of existing equipment and objectives of the landlord.

Core Concepts

✓ Tenant handbook
✓ Crisis management manual and catastrophe planning

COMMUNICATION WITH TENANT

A vital part of any successful maintenance program is a partnership between the landlord and the tenants. An open channel of communication between the landlord and tenant (your customer) provides more efficient equipment upkeep. For example, if a leak develops in the roof of a store, immediate contact between the tenant and the center manager can solve the problem before it becomes a major concern.

Communication is established at the signing of a lease, and all salient issues should be reviewed in detail with the tenant.

Two other booklets also define tenant/landlord communications:

1. The welcome book, sometimes referred to as a tenant hand-book: A guide that introduces the tenant to the rules and

regulations of the shopping center. It also provides information on such things as:

—Community services available to the tenant

—Emergency service telephone numbers

—Names and phone numbers of management staff

—Management goals and philosophy.

2. The emergency book: A crisis-management guide for a tenant to follow in the event of an emergency or accident. The booklet may contain information on:

—Emergency services telephone numbers

—Management contact in case of emergency

—Crowd control and evacuation procedures

—How to secure store operations, such as shutting off gas or electrical systems for their premises

—Guidelines to follow in case of natural disasters such as earthquakes or floods.

There are other procedures a center manager can implement to ensure a smooth relationship with tenants:

- Budget estimates give the tenant an idea of how much maintenance will cost in a given year.
- Scheduling informs the tenant about planned renovation work and gives advance warning to prepare for possible business disruption.
- Prompt response, follow-through and courtesy make tenants feel part of the center.

Core Concepts:

✓ Timing of inspections
✓ Equipment warranty
✓ Emergency repairs
✓ Coordinating work with tenants

SCHEDULING OF INSPECTIONS AND MAINTENANCE

The lease document and the *Standard Operating Procedures Manual* will dictate the frequency of inspection. Among the options:

- Inspections are usually done on either a standard or an annual basis. A standard inspection is a daily, weekly or monthly inspection.
- A full-site inspection by the maintenance manager may be made either monthly or every other month, depending upon the condition of a shopping center.
- Certain products and systems will require daily inspections. For example, rest rooms in common areas should be

inspected daily or even hourly to see if cleaning is needed or that cleaning has been done.

■ Certain products and procedures will require different times of day or year for a proper inspection. For example, due to the principles of expansion and contraction, cracks in asphalt parking lots are more noticeable when the temperature is cool.

■ Maintenance schedules stipulated in warranties should be complied with.

■ Insurance policies must be complied with in order for policies to maintain their warranty.

The schedule for a repair project may hinge on the properties of the asset being fixed. Other things to consider include:

■ Not postponing emergency repairs until ideal weather conditions. For example, a pothole formed in winter should still be repaired. It is understood that the solution is temporary and that permanent work will be done during ideal conditions.

■ Not scheduling major repair work during retailers' peak sales times.

■ Letting the tenants know well in advance of any major repair work. They may want to know (1) what type of repair work is going on, (2) how the work is going to be done, (3) how long it will take and (4) the effect the work will have on them.

Core Concepts

✓ In-house and contract maintenance
✓ Maintenance hours allocation by tasks
✓ Other costs

FOUNDATION OF THE MAINTENANCE DEPARTMENT

E ach center's maintenance and housekeeping depart-
ments will vary in size and skill level depending on the
size and complexity of the shopping center. Management
must balance the requirement to maintain the building according to the leases, REAs and owner's standards with the cost to
operate and implement those systems. Staffing for the various
functions can be divided into three categories:

- Totally staffed by in-house personnel
- Totally staffed by outsourcing the personnel with contrac-
  tors
- A combination of the two

In determining the approach that management wants to take in staffing and implementing the maintenance and housekeeping functions of the shopping center, it is important to compare costs by evaluating in-house costs first. Consider the following criteria:

- Personnel staffing requirement (based on total hours needed rather than by number of forty-hour/week people)
- Employee benefits
- Cost of supplies and materials, including any up-front capital costs, with depreciation over three years
- Uniform costs
- Training costs
- Workers' compensation insurance
- Administration time involved in handling personnel matters and paperwork
- Manager's time involved in hiring and terminations
- Turnover
- Americans with Disabilities Act (ADA) compliance

Once you have considered these issues, you need to address some of the following questions:

- What is your core business or responsibility as the manager of the center? What does ownership want you to emphasize? Evaluate the time that is needed to accomplish these tasks.
- What is the employment/labor market in your area? Is there high or low unemployment?
- Are the tasks that need to be performed of a specialized nature or of an infrequent time frame? You could just pay for that service one time rather than carry the payroll year-round. For instance, do you want to buy and maintain snow removal equipment year-round to be used for

just two or three snowfalls a year? Yet you may be in an area where snowfall is a major factor and where maintaining the equipment is a necessity, as there is a limited supply of companies that can provide services to you because they are needed to maintain the major roadways.

■ What will it cost in payroll dollars to hire the expertise to manage or oversee certain maintenance functions, such as landscaping, pest control and insecticide application?

■ Is there growth opportunity for your staff, so as to avoid turnover?

■ Is your company willing to train and develop the personnel at your site to keep up with the latest technologies?

■ Does the location/market of your center prevent outsourcing companies from wanting to or being able to travel to your center?

■ What are ownership's goals and objectives for the property?

■ How do you balance the need to achieve the goals and objectives versus managing personnel?

■ Is the property a real estate investment trust (REIT) or is it privately owned? Properties in REIT tend to be more income driven, thus ownership may demand that you concentrate on income-producing efforts rather than managing personnel.

■ Do the size and the sales volume of the center allow you to maintain skilled in-house personnel and still focus on your core goals and objectives?

■ Due to the high visibility of your property, may outsourcing companies price their services lower just to say that the center is their customer—a form of advertisement for them?

After you calculate the above numbers and dollars, you can

determine which course of action to take. The most common approach is a combination of in-house staff and outsourcing of services. There is no one answer as to which services should be handled in-house and which services should be outsourced.

Core Concepts

✓ Cleaning standards
✓ Daily vs. monthly inspections
✓ Exterior landscaping

TASKS PERFORMED IN KEY MAINTENANCE AREAS

Janitorial/Cleaning

One of the most defining areas that sets various shopping centers apart is the quality of the housekeeping at the center. To understand how to maintain a cleaning standard that is acceptable to the tenants and customers, management must have a detailed set of procedures for the staff to follow. Of utmost importance is the need for management to inspect daily the interior and exterior common areas before the center opens for business. Management must have a diligent routine of walking and inspecting the exterior grounds, truck docks, parking areas, back hallways, rest rooms, fountains, doors, windows, tenant storefronts and trash cans. This will assure the manager that the center is ready for customers and the environment is free of any hazards.

Also, management must provide tasks each day to the housekeeping staff. For example, daily tasks could include emptying all trash containers, clearing all truck docks of debris, cleaning all center door windows before 9 A.M., policing and picking up litter from the common area parking lot and cleaning all rest room fixtures. Nightly tasks could include scrubbing and mopping the center's common area walkways and food court floors, wiping down and cleaning all chairs and tables, cleaning all trash cans, pressure washing all entrance ways and removing all gum, drinks, spills and so on. Daily tasks in the food court could include washing and cleaning all tables and chairs within the seating area, checking and emptying all trash cans on a regular basis, cleaning and returning all food trays to the respective tenants and mopping all spills immediately.

General Maintenance

It is also very important to check the operating status of all items within the center on a daily basis. Each maintenance staff member should have routines to follow. This will assure management that the building is being maintained and that no item is neglected. If operational problems are neglected, they can become safety hazards and/or liability issues as well as major expenditures. Following are suggested items the maintenance staff should have scheduled rounds to inspect and repair, among others.

Daily:
- Inspect rest rooms and make sure fixtures are running properly.

- Inspect and repair all door handles, hinges, glass, closures, etc., including public entrances and service entrance doors.
- Check and clean out all water fountains within the common area.
- Check for broken irrigation fixtures to prevent water waste.
- Check the parking lot for potholes, broken curbs, etc. Have security check the parking and building lights nightly to ensure that none are out and no safety hazards exist.
- Check for any safety hazards. These include broken tiles, torn carpet, cracks in the sidewalk, etc.
- When it snows, lay down chemicals at entranceways to prevent slips and falls each day. Change floor mats, as they become wet and dirty during heavy snowfall days.

Monthly:
- Check the roof for debris left by outside workers.
- Check all common area HVAC units and replace filters. Perform the preventive maintenance program as outlined.
- Check all fire extinguishers and smoke alarms.
- Caution: When buying and placing plant containers, be aware of ADA requirements. You do not want to create a traffic hazard for people going through the mall.

Exterior Landscaping. One of the first impressions that a customer has of your center is the exterior landscaping. The appearance and maintenance of your exterior landscaping send a signal to your customers and tenants that your property is a place to come to and stay in awhile. It softens the feel of all the exterior asphalt in the parking lot. It can hide building flaws. It can announce mall entrances. It can provide color and greenery to an otherwise poor architectural design. But landscaping needs to be planned and maintained in a way that will not create liability or unusual maintenance problems.

Only consider those plants and trees that are common to the geographic region. You need to consider the weather conditions, the amount of rainfall and the amount of snowfall. Keep trees away from parking lot light poles. At nighttime, they can create liability issues. Avoid trees whose roots are shallow. These can cause eruptions in your parking lot and create additional liability issues from trips and falls. Avoid dirty trees, such as ones that create berries that may damage the paint on cars. Create barriers around tree islands so that snow removal equipment does not damage your landscaping. Keep trees pruned above eight feet to avoid dangerous limbs. Watch for dead tree limbs that can fall and injure customers or damage cars.

Core Concepts

✓ Return on investment (ROI)
✓ Replace vs. repair

EQUIPMENT REPLACEMENT

Parameters for the repair or replacement of a malfunctioning asset are part of most shopping centers' maintenance packages.

Return on investment (ROI) is an analysis used to determine the value of an existing asset to a shopping center. An evaluation of the final figure determines if equipment should be repaired or replaced. There are many ways to evaluate ROI data. Generally, the more expensive an asset is to maintain, the more likely it is to be replaced instead of repaired. For example, a standard ROI is to compare yearly maintenance cost and the price of new equipment. If maintenance exceeds half the replacement price, the landlord will often choose to replace the asset in question. In addition to the ROI, a landlord should consider the following factors:

- The lease: Under certain clauses, the tenant, not the landlord, pays for replacement of failed equipment.
- Necessity: Sometimes, in order to ensure the well-being of the entire shopping center, a landlord will be forced to pay for the replacement of an entire asset. For example, if a roof fails after a storm, the landlord will have to replace it immediately.

Reasons to Repair Instead of Replace

- Short-term rehabilitation: The landlord of a center about to undergo a major renovation may opt to temporarily repair a malfunctioning asset instead of replacing it.
- Budget restraints: Repair is usually less expensive than replacement. Landlords and managers on a tight budget often choose to repair for this reason.

Reasons to Replace Instead of Repair

- Greater efficiency: Replacement of old equipment with newer, energy-efficient models can save money.
- Aesthetic appeal: Occasionally, new equipment is substituted for old to improve the atmosphere of a center. For example, the replacement of faded awnings makes an older center more attractive.
- Safety: Assets decayed to the point of being hazardous should be replaced to avoid liability—for example, replacement of burned-out bulbs in a parking lot.
- Check for incentives from your local utility providers, which may offset the cost of more energy-efficient equipment.

Core Concepts

✓ CAPEX
✓ CAM recoverable vs. landlord expense
✓ Administrative fees
✓ Management fees

THE BUDGET

The budget for shopping center maintenance is constructed on a yearly basis. However, separate budgets will be needed for certain projects. When calculating the cost of these projects, keep in mind:

- Cost of maintenance procedures will run the gamut, depending upon (1) what needs to be maintained or fixed and (2) in what part of the country the shopping center is located.

- Labor costs are usually the wild card of the budget process, and provisions must be made accordingly. For example, prices for products involved in roof replacement can be found out by the supplier and an accurate budget calculated from the price quotes. Labor costs to replace the roof will, however, vary greatly from region to region and with the difficulty of the work involved. Most budget errors stem from incorrect assumptions of labor costs.

Capital Expense

Most maintenance for the common area falls under CAM and can be charged to the tenant. However, structural work done to a center may be considered a capital expense (CAPEX) if funds are used to acquire or upgrade physical assets such as buildings or machinery beyond its original condition. Payments for capital expenses are often the responsibility of the landlord, although this will vary greatly from center to center, depending on the lease. The accounting department will determine if an expense should be capitalized (spread through several years) or expensed during one year. The lease, not how the expense is treated accounting-wise, is the controlling document that determines if the expense is recoverable as CAM or the responsibility of the landlord.

Examples of a capital expense may include:

- Replacement of HVAC machinery
- Reconstruction of a storm sewer system.

Some examples of CAM charges are:

- Landscaping
- Parking lot lighting
- Snow removal.

CAM is usually charged monthly and adjusted yearly. To compute monthly CAM for tenants, most shopping centers use the following formula: Divide the estimated annual budget by 12 and adjust to the true cost at the end of the year. For example, if the estimated yearly CAM for a center is $120,000 and the tenant's space represents 10% of the GLA, then the monthly CAM fee will be $1,000. If at year end CAM totals $121,000, the tenant will be billed an extra $100.

Times of payment will fluctuate depending upon the type of lease signed. For example, some leases stipulate CAM payment on a quarterly basis. However, most leases are designed to have a tenant pay monthly estimated and adjusted annually, as mentioned above.

Offsets

On rare occasions, percentage rent is offset against the CAM payments. For example, a tenant's CAM charge is $10,000. However, the tenant owes an additional $1,200 in rent because sales surpass a negotiated limit and percentage rent kicks in. A very few leases allow the tenant to subtract percentage rent from CAM, so in this scenario the tenant owes the center $8,800. Offsets will vary greatly from lease to lease.

Administrative and Management Fees

Depending on specific lease language, both administrative fees and management fees are calculated into CAM.

- The administrative fee is calculated from a negotiated percentage of the total CAM budget for a center. For example, if the total CAM for a shopping center is $300,000, and the administrative percentage is set at 10%, the fee will be $30,000.
- The management fee typically is a percentage of the gross collectibles of a center. The gross collectible of a center is

the total amount of all the money collected from tenants for CAM, percentage rent, minimum rent and taxes. For example, if the collectible for a center is $1 million and the management fee is set at 5%, the sum owed the center management would be $50,000. By contrast with administrative fees that are typically included in CAM, the management fee is not typically included in CAM.

- Although not considered standard, few leases include real estate taxes in CAM and many leases include common area insurance expenses in CAM. The administrative charge in this case may then be applied to the entire expense. The lease agreement between the landlord and tenant dictate what charges are to be included as CAM and how administrative charges are computed.

Core Concepts

✓ Work done on the roof: HVAC, antenna

✓ Roof terminology: Built-up roofs, single ply, felt, bitumen

✓ Roof inspections for signs of failure

ROOF MAINTENANCE

Roof maintenance can be one of the most neglected aspects of shopping center management and ownership. The roof is out of sight, and oftentimes out of mind—until there is a roof leak. Not only are roof leaks unsightly, but they can increase your liability insurance due to slips and falls in the common area. How does a good shopping center maintenance program prevent and anticipate roof repair needs? By having someone walk the roof on a regular basis, all four seasons of the year. Some thoughts on roof maintenance and how to keep the major costs at bay follow:

- No roof bond or guarantee keeps water out of a building.
- The number one cause of failure is poor workmanship during installation.

- The number two cause of failure is inadequate maintenance.

- When making your routine inspections, note any splits, bubbles, low spots, blocked drains and new penetrations such as antennas, fan ducts, satellite dishes, etc.

- The roofing system is a major factor in the energy consumption of any shopping center.

- Roof drains need to be inspected monthly to ensure that they are free of debris to allow for quick drainage during and after rainfall.

- HVAC repair workers are one of the major causes of roof problems. They often do not pick up discarded tools, screws, trash and other types of materials that can wreak havoc on your roofing system, especially on a single-ply roofing system.

In its most basic form, a roof is a waterproofing device, a membrane designed to keep moisture from entering the premises. There are many different types of roofs, usually determined by:

- The kind of material used or
- The way the material is applied.

For example, a single-ply roof is made out of one layer of plastic or rubber sheeting adhered to a roofing deck, while a built-up roof is made up of combined layers of felt and bitumens (either coal tar pitch or asphalt-based by-products of the oil-to-gasoline production process).

The most common type of roof for large shopping centers remains built-up (described below). However, a large number of alternative roofing surfaces have appeared over the last few years. Often, specifications such as roof slope, load bearing or design will force the use of an alternative style, among them:

- Single ply
- Modified bitumen
- Metal
- Rubber
- Glass or plastic (skylights).

Built-Up Roofs (BURs)

A BUR consists of the following items:

- Deck: This is the prepared surface on which the roof is laid. It usually consists of metal, wood or concrete.
- Insulation: In the case of a BUR, rigid fiberboard on fiberglass is usually the material of choice. Other vapor retarders may be used in colder climates.
- Roof membrane: The waterproofing system that usually consists of felts with moppings of bitumen in between. Felts come in various weights and are classified in terms of pounds, that is, 15 lbs. or 20 lbs. Felts provide the tensile strength. The number of felt layers, called plies, determines the overall strength of a roof. For example, a four-ply roof is twice as strong as a two-ply roof, all other considerations being equal.

A BUR is created when felts are joined to a deck and each other by bitumens or some other form of adhesion. Usually the roof is then coated with a protective surface, such as gravel. A drainage system is placed to move water off the roof. A membrane and all its protective and water-moving devices is called a roof system.

Failure

A roof fails when it leaks. The origin of a leak can be either natural or man-made. Some man-made causes of roof failure are:

- Improper product or placement of product: For example, adhering coal tar felts with asphalt bitumen will cause roof problems. Match the right bitumen with the proper type of felt.
- Bad design: For example, a roof with too few drains will pool water. Standing water is a primary cause of roof failure.
- Improperly trained installers: Inexperienced crews may make mistakes. For example, if not enough bitumen is mopped onto a felt-ply, it will eventually delaminate and leak.
- Unsupervised installation: Mistakes may occur when installation takes place without inspection. For example, the temperature of the bitumen used to coat a roof needs to be carefully monitored. Too hot or too cold an application of bitumen will produce a poor roof.
- Lack of inspection: Failure on the landlord's part to inspect roofs. For example, failure to clear debris from rain gutters leads to standing water on the roof and eventual leaks.
- Unsupervised access to roof: Any penetration of the roofing membrane can cause a leak. For example, a tenant who goes up on a roof, without permission, to install a television antenna and nails it directly to the roof may accidentally cause damage.

Avoiding Failure

Proper installation goes a long way in alleviating roof failure. The keys to proper roof placement are:

- Quality materials
- Trained installers
- Proper plans and planning
- Regular inspection.

Other keys to roof longevity include:

- Monthly inspection
- Efficient maintenance
- Access control: The fewer people on the roof, the less chance for accidental penetration. Supervise any work crew that goes on the roof.
- Limit membrane penetration: Man-made holes put in the roof for skylights, HVAC units, etc., can leak. Avoid penetrating the roof surface whenever possible.

Inspection

A management-supervised roof inspection should take place at least four times a year. However, many managers walk the roof at least once a month. For a major roofing job, consider the use of an expert or factory representative for inspection. Certain nuances, such as measurement of kettle temperatures and proper thickness of bitumen between plies, can only be ascertained by professionals.

In summary, if you have an effective roof management program, you can lower your life-cycle roofing costs significantly. Your demand for emergency leak repairs should be drastically reduced. You should then be able to project your specific needs and budgets on an annual basis with very few surprises. You will require less labor and less money to perform the roofing management function over time.

Core Concepts

✓ HVAC terminology: thermostats, central plant, chilled water, cooling tower, packaged units

✓ HVAC capacity/tonnage, heat discharge and heat load calculations

✓ Maintenance after installation

HEATING, VENTILATION AND AIR CONDITIONING (HVAC) SYSTEM

While janitorial and landscaping services can set the standard for the appearance of your property, the quality of the environment which your customers and tenants experience depends on the quality of your HVAC maintenance program. In today's building design, conditioning the environment in the building is becoming a much more important aspect of building management. Issues such as "sick building syndrome," climate control for indoor plants and control of energy costs are all related to the maintenance of your HVAC system.

The type of HVAC systems within shopping centers is usually

based on the age, location and type of building. For example, some centers have central plant equipment in which the air-conditioning and heating are controlled out of a central location and supplied to the tenants and common area through a piping system via chilled water or steam heat. In this system, large air handlers move the air through the cooled coils to distribute air-conditioning. As the chilled water is warmed by this cycle, the water is cooled down in a cooling tower, then sent back to the chillers in the central plant to cool all over again before it reaches the coils to be again blown by the air handlers. In some areas, gas may be used for heating if it is available and cost-efficient. Some centers utilize individual package units, as opposed to a central plant, which provide the heating and air-conditioning for both the tenants and the common areas.

No matter what the system, there are a few basic items that every manager needs to keep in mind:

- The number one cause of air-conditioning compressor failure is dirty air filters. The second is loose belts.
- Replacing any HVAC equipment more than twelve years old is generally a good investment since you will have reduced maintenance costs and increased energy efficiency.
- Keep thermostats away from high customer traffic areas and inaccessible to employees. Everyone loves to play with thermostats and no two people have the same air-conditioning needs. An automatic energy management system is one alternative.
- Establish preventive maintenance programs for HVAC equipment. Regular maintenance pays off in reliable operations, fewer breakdowns and longer life. Evaluate your program from time to time and make any required modifications.

- Know the brand of your HVAC equipment. All brands have certain idiosyncrasies that require special attention in certain areas.
- If you are outsourcing, be sure the contractor is performing as contracted.
- Be aware of the pending Environmental Protection Agency (EPA) rules as they relate to the use of various refrigerants known under such brand names as Freon, Genetron and Isotron.
- Be willing to pay the price for quality HVAC preventive maintenance programs. There is nothing more disconcerting to a tenant or a customer than being too cold during the winter months or too hot during the summer months due to HVAC breakdowns.
- HVAC equipment is also classified by tonnage of air or British thermal units (BTUs). A BTU is the amount of heat required to raise one pound of water one degree Fahrenheit. A ton of air is 12,000 BTUs. The tonnage or BTU capacity of an HVAC system determines its capacity. The greater the tonnage, the greater the capacity for heating and cooling.

Installation

The tonnage of the HVAC system needed by a center or store space is determined by the size of the sales area. The following general formula is used to compute HVAC need:

400–450 square feet of sales area = 1 ton of air

The following factors should also be taken into consideration:

- Lighting: Heat discharged from display lighting affects HVAC requirements. For example, for every 450 square feet of sales space in a store, one ton of HVAC air is required. However, if a clothing store has three display lighting systems that have high footcandle readings, the landlord may want to readjust and have one ton of air for every 300–350 square feet of space in this store.

- Type of merchandise: Soft goods require a higher percentage of HVAC air than other types of merchandise. For example, a men's fashion outlet will need more HVAC coverage than a housewares store.

- Subdivisions: Stores that are subdivided into many smaller rooms or have false ceilings, changing cubicles, back-office space and storage rooms disrupt the flow and cycle of air around a leased space and will require more air tonnage per square foot. Firms that specialize in balancing HVAC systems can often optimize efficiency.

- Food service: Stores with kitchens and other hot areas will require higher HVAC coverage to offset heat and odor.

- Change of tenant: HVAC tonnage may need to be changed with the arrival of a new tenant. For example, a food court space originally designed to handle an ice cream store may need more HVAC tonnage if a fast food merchandiser moves into the space.

- Heat load calculations for any new tenant should be reviewed to determine the HVAC capacity of the space. Additional tonnage may be required. For instance, a high heat load jewelry store requires more conditioned air than a regular retail tenant. Extra HVAC cost should be passed on to the new tenant.

Inspection and Maintenance

Management-supervised HVAC upkeep is important for a number of reasons:

- Access control: Management-supervised inspection and maintenance helps to keep unauthorized people away from equipment. It also lessens the potential for accidental roof damage.
- Cost savings: Generally, it is cheaper to have all HVAC units maintained by one contractor rather than have each retailer use its own contractor to maintain its unit. However, in most cases this is a tenant responsibility with individual retailer costs being the retailer's issue only.
- Skilled maintenance: The center manager can make certain that only experienced workers handle HVAC equipment.
- Documentation: Better record-keeping results from centralized HVAC upkeep and environmental requirements.
- Lease requirements: If tenants maintain equipment, assurance of maintenance programs and evidence of contractor's insurance coverage are required.

Core Concepts

✓ Parking lot resurfacing and repair

✓ Terminology: subgrade, asphalt lifts, potholes, sealers, coal tar, slurry, emulsion

✓ Parking deck concerns for lighting and safety

PARKING SURFACES

Asphalt

Asphalt is the surface material of most roadways and parking lots surrounding shopping centers. Asphalt maintenance is almost always the responsibility of the shopping center manager.

Installation

Asphalt parking lot or roadway construction involves the following distinct steps:

- Subgrade preparation: The subgrade is the base of a parking lot or roadway. It is the prepared surface on which asphalt is laid. Factors such as use and traffic will influence subgrade constitution and thickness.

- Asphalt lifts: Asphalt is laid on a prepared subgrade in two cycles called lifts. The first lift is generally done for contouring, the development of slope and drainage. The second lift adds compaction and creates thickness.
- Sealers: After asphalt has been placed and cured, a sealer is often applied to the surface to provide protection and add aesthetic appeal. The most common types of sealer are coal tar, slurry and asphalt emulsion. Which one an owner chooses depends on such factors as cost, look and protection.

Other keys to proper asphalt installation include:

- Drainage: Water penetration is the number one cause leading to failed parking lots and roadways.
- Thickness: Proper thickness will vary depending upon roadway use.
- Temperature: The ideal weather temperature for asphalt is between 70 and 80 degrees Fahrenheit.
- Curbing: Curbs that have solid foundations established below grade level last longer than those designed to sit on the surface (referred to as constructed curbing)
- Inspection: Testing procedures such as taking core samples will enable you to determine compacted thickness, size of rock and materials used. These procedures should be performed by an experienced engineer.

Parking Lots

One of the most neglected areas of shopping center maintenance is the parking lot. Daily inspection of the parking lot is needed and items of note should be attended to immediately, otherwise they can become major expenditures or result in major liability claims. Items that should be noted in an inspection are:

- Faded, broken or vandalized traffic signs
- Faded or hard-to-see traffic directional markings on the drive lanes
- Broken curbing and broken car stops that could create accidents and tripping hazards
- Potholes in drive lanes that need to be repaired before they become a major expense or create a liability
- Policing and picking up broken glass, bottles and cans daily can reduce wear and tear on the asphalt and can prevent customers from tripping over such items.
- Small cracks in the asphalt should be attended to immediately. These cracks should be cleaned out and sealed before they become major potholes.
- Parking lot striping should be done once a year, depending on the location of your center. Keep the striping and traffic directional signals easy to see.

Parking Decks

To meet parking space requirements specified in REA agreements with the tenants and to meet local code regulations, owners are adding parking decks. While parking decks allow for protection from weather conditions such as rain, heat and snow, they do present unique problems. Lighting and safety concerns are uppermost in the minds of the customers and the tenants. Review lighting, patrols and call-box needs in this area. Traffic control signage should be highly visible and easy to read. Areas should be marked to help customers remember where they parked their cars. Pedestrian walkways and safety islands should be well lit and noted.

Core Concepts

✓ Specifications in contract
✓ Response time

SNOW REMOVAL

Very few centers maintain their own snow removal equipment, due to the capital outlay and cost of personnel. Outsourcing the work, either fully or partially, is the typical practice among property managers. Planning ahead is the key. It is important to lay out the timing and procedures for when and how snow removal will be done, as well as where to dump the snow. Prior to executing the contract, walk the property with your contractor. Identify existing curbs, signs, landscaping, speed bumps and damage in the parking lot. Contracts should note which roadways and areas should be cleared first and where to store the accumulated snow. Negotiate an agreement that is tailored to your locale and customer base.

Develop a price that will provide for a standby fee plus an hourly rate on each piece of equipment. The contract should also specify an automatic response time, a minimum level of service under specified conditions and an additional price as directed.

> # Core Concepts
>
> ✓ Foot candles
> ✓ Group relamping for efficiencies

LIGHTING SYSTEMS MAINTENANCE

Exterior Lighting Systems

The perception of safety in a parking lot is directly related to the *amount of light that parking lot light poles emit.* Shopping center managers should constantly monitor the number of *inoperable lamps* in a lot at any one time and make replacements promptly. Keep detailed records of each pole and when the lightbulb ballast are replaced. *Clean the light fixture lenses* to increase light levels. Determine the safest and most convenient time to turn off lights after evening center closing in accordance with tenant and customer needs. Lighting is measured in candlepower per square foot. Distance between poles can affect average foot candles. Total lighting in parking

---

lots and parking decks can contribute to a safety perception. High pressure sodium, mercury vapor, and fluorescent lighting are among lighting types used in the exterior and interior of shopping centers. A maintenance supervisor should be aware of the types of lighting outputs and energy efficiencies of each type of lighting.

Interior Lighting Systems

Planned lighting and group relamping maintenance programs provide the shopping center manager with cost controls and uniform lighting levels throughout the center. Most planned lighting and maintenance programs consist of three elements:

- *group relampings*
- *repair services*
- *emergency response provisions*

It is important to schedule the mass replacement of aging and inefficient lamps not only before they fail, but when lighting levels degrade over time.

Core Concepts

✓ Know the type of plants used
✓ Treat for disease and insects
✓ Qualified contractors

INTERIOR LANDSCAPING

Proper landscaping maintenance can distinguish your shopping center from the rest of the competition. Yet if it is not kept up, the appearance of the landscape can have a deterrent effect on your customers.

When evaluating your interior landscaping program, some of the basic elements to be considered are as follows:

- Potted landscape plants can define seating areas without developing permanent barriers.
- Keep the plants clean, free of dust and insects, and properly cared for.
- Avoid high and dense plants in front of storefronts, as this will block the visibility of the tenants' signs.

- Potted plants can be used to reduce liability by creating natural barriers around architectural designs and to signal changes in elevations within walkways.

- Usually annual (or tropical) plants and shrubs are used in the interior of shopping centers as well as trees that don't shed. Seasonal flowers are brought in for contrast, e.g., poinsettias in November, mums in early spring.

- Plants are living things preferably cared for by qualified contractors that will water, feed, trim and replace as necessary.

Core Concepts

✓ Emergency generator timer and fuel

✓ Service contractors for vertical transportation

✓ Emergency repairs on elevators and escalators

MECHANICAL AND ELECTRICAL

Some of the more complex systems in a shopping center are its mechanical and electrical components requiring care and preventive maintenance.

Emergency Generators

There should be a timer on the emergency generator so that it is exercised on a regular basis, specifically on weekly intervals. The tank should be checked on a weekly basis to determine its fuel level. Detailed written logs should be kept and, once a history is developed, regular prescheduled refills of fuel can be arranged with the local supplier.

Electrical Systems

Emergency generators are typically located in truck docks and are fueled either by natural gas or diesel. The supply is usually contained either in a nearby underground storage tank if it is diesel, or in a direct line if it is natural gas. There should be a timer on the emergency generator so that it is exercised on a regular basis at specified intervals. This is one maintenance task that the manager should oversee to ensure that the scheduled log is maintained and to prevent failure in an emergency.

In the case of parking lot lighting, a *backup system* must be in place to respond to a power outage. In addition to having parts and materials in stock and readily available, designation of an on-call electrical service company or a company from which temporary lights can be ordered to supplement the regular parking lot lights until they are repaired is an essential component of managing a center's electrical system.

Elevators and Escalators

It is imperative that the manager deal only with reliable service companies. These companies should have access to and maintain an adequate supply of key parts on hand, as well as certified technicians to work on the center's specific brand of equipment. Additionally, the manager must be assured that the service is capable and is staffed to respond to emergencies during business hours, as well as after the center closes.

Core Concepts

✓ Key terminology: trays, tables, chairs, trash receptacles, grease traps

✓ Health department compliance

FOOD COURT

Managing a food court involves a diverse set of responsibilities. Among the key areas of supervision are housekeeping, maintenance, budgets, and tenant relations. Depending on the specific shopping center, a manager may also oversee such areas as lease enforcement, labor, supplies (such as *food trays and cleansers*), equipment (such as *tables, chairs and lighting fixtures*), insurance, security, and marketing and publicity.

Daily cleaning and the ongoing upkeep of the food court are important areas of supervision for the food court manager because of the health aspect of food service and because diners are sensitive to appearances when eating.

Food grease, steam, odors, and stains; smoke from grills and pits; melted ice cream; and spilled condiments on floors are among the cleaning issues that combine to complicate the cleanliness of the food court. Food courts also require special cleaning procedures and cleansers such as *disinfectants and degreasers.* Grease traps should be serviced periodically.

Food courts need to have an adequate *supply of trash receptacles,* which must be emptied frequently and cleaned thoroughly. All surfaces, such as *countertops or display cases,* should be cleaned on a regular basis, as they easily show finger and hand prints.

Core Concepts

✓ Electricity, gas, water, sewer
✓ Utility companies

UTILITIES

Many of the utilities in shopping centers will be supplied by utility companies or by the county or other local governments. Each supplier of a utility will require an *easement for the installation and ongoing maintenance of such utility.* It will not be uncommon for the representatives of the local utility company to deal directly with the shopping center manager in connection with easements. Typical utilities are electricity, gas, water and sewer.

Core Concepts

✓ Post policy
✓ Service drains
✓ Qualified contractor

PLUMBING SYSTEMS

A consistent program for monitoring tenant use of the plumbing system is important to the avoidance of stoppages. Management should first set a policy regarding what may be disposed in the system and post that information for display in all tenant storerooms and restrooms. Depending on where any problems occur, a *regular routing program* should be in place to eliminate blockages. Restaurants must implement a regularly scheduled maintenance program for *cleaning drains* and grease traps. A special timer should be placed on all water systems that feed the disposal system; it must operate the water for a period of time after the disposal system stops.

Mall drains should be placed on a regular chemical and routing maintenance schedule. A qualified plumbing contractor should be available on an emergency basis at any time of the day.

INFORMATION TECHNOLOGY

Remain current on existing and new systems to maximize leasing, financial reporting, and maintenance systems.

Core Concepts

✓ Common area trash removal

✓ Compactors and dumpsters

✓ Trash hauling to landfill

✓ Recycling is a responsibility often mandated by law

✓ Environmental concerns

WASTE MANAGEMENT

The property manager and maintenance supervisor are responsible for the *removal of trash from the common areas.* Depending on the lease provisions, either the tenants or the property manager may be responsible for contracting for the removal of the tenants' trash. Major tenants usually contract for the removal of their own trash. Some tenants may have individual trash receptacles and contract directly with a trash-hauling company. More often tenants use a central compactor and dumpster, and the property manager contracts for trash removal from the center to a landfill, known as "trash hauling." If all the tenants use central trash dumpsters, the trash removal may be a CAM expense.

Recycling

Center management collects recyclable material from tenants and shoppers in several ways. When recycling cardboard, the shopping center owner may *purchase or lease a compactor that bales cardboard for all the other tenants,* who usually do not generate sufficient cardboard to justify buying their own balers. The lease payment for the compactor would be a CAM expense, since the savings on the trash pickup reduce CAM expenses and revenue received for the cardboard is credited against the CAM expense.

If it is not practical to purchase or lease a compactor, the property manager may arrange with a *recycling company* to pick up flattened or unflattened boxes from each store and, with another firm, to pick up packaging materials from the tenants. The manager may also *install containers for glass, plastic, newspapers, and aluminum recycling.* Installing community recycling containers also provides a valuable service and creates good will for the shopping center manager. Another option is to allow a recycling company to install a machine that returns deposits for empty cans.

The property manager is the key person to coordinate a *recycling program* and must be aware of the five components of such a program's success: (1) obtain the support of the tenants; (2) work with maintenance and recycling contractors to implement the program; (3) develop the recycling program; (4) continually educate the tenants and promote the program; and (5) monitor and report on the success of the recycling program. Sometimes recycling is mandated by law.

Environmental Services

Asbestos abatement is a phased program to remove all asbestos-containing materials from the center. This is of particular concern where there is a planned demolition and/or renovation of a portion of a shopping center in which asbestos and *asbestos-containing materials (ACMs)* might be disturbed.

Chlorofluorocarbons (CFCs) are an ozone-depleting compound utilized by some HVAC units manufactured before 1995. The U.S. Federal Clean Air Act provides among other things that as of 1995 manufacturers of air conditioners and other appliances are prohibited from producing equipment that emits ozone-deleting compounds.

Contaminants are substances that are strictly forbidden to be mixed with trash or recycling when disposing of them. There are many types classified as hazardous wastes substances by federal or state/province law, which must be disposed of by a qualified and licensed environmental hauler in a manner prescribed by law.

Be aware of all environmental laws, rules, and regulations on federal, state and province or local levels that govern so-called hazardous materials. Perhaps the best known is the comprehensive *Environmental Response, Compensation and Liability Act* (CERCLA), commonly known as the Superfund Act, which includes detailed definitions of *"hazard substances"* and establishes rules for determining who is responsible for cleaning up or remediating a site which has been contaminated by hazardous substances. Examples of hazard substances are *dry-cleaning chemicals; gasoline and other petroleum-based prod-*

ucts as well as asbestos. The shopping center manager must take reasonable steps to monitor the condition of the property in order to *quickly identify contamination and to limit the effects thereof.*

Core Concepts

✓ Lighting inspection
✓ Obstruction by overgrown landscaping
✓ Emergency exit lights
✓ Vandalism evidence

SECURITY MAINTENANCE

Property managers may inspect their properties as often as once per month or as little as once per year. The frequency depends on several factors, such as the property's age, condition, and location. During the *maintenance inspection*, the property manager looks for both maintenance and security issues such as overgrown landscaping, poor lighting, and graffiti or evidence of vandalism. At least one inspection should be conducted during the evening, when the common area lights are on. The manager should also review the *property's emergency procedures* periodically and change them as necessary.

Core Concepts

✓ ADA, OSHA

✓ Environmental concerns: dry cleaners, underground storage tanks (UST)

SPECIAL MAINTENANCE ISSUES

There are a number of special maintenance issues that a manager needs to be aware of as they relate to the operation of the center:

1. *The Americans with Disabilities Act (ADA) Compliance Regulations.* The act, signed by the first President Bush in July 1990, is designed to extend civil rights protection to persons with disabilities. The law is divided into five major titles that prohibit discrimination against the disabled in employment, state and local government services, public transportation, public accommodations and telecommunications. The two titles that have the greatest impact on operations and maintenance of shopping centers are public accommodations and telecommunications. Under public ac-

commodations, persons with disabilities are to be provided accommodations and access equal to, or similar to, that which is available to the general public.

2. *Roof management tools.* Infrared imaging can be used to locate wet materials within the roof system by providing a visual representation of heat radiated from the roof.

3. *Refrigerant certification.* Make sure that your contractor is certified under the EPA certification test.

4. *Clean Air Act.* This relates to boilers on the property. The Clean Air Act was enacted to regulate and reduce air pollution. The Clean Air Act is administered by the U.S. Environmental Protection Agency.

5. *Clean Water Act.* This relates to storm water drainage and runoff of the shopping center's parking lot. Are there catch basins in place to contain contaminants?

6. *Occupational Safety and Health Administration (OSHA).* OSHA was created to encourage employers to reduce workplace hazards, to implement new or to improve existing safety and health programs, to develop mandatory job safety and health standards, to enforce these standards in the workplace and to maintain a reporting and record keeping system to monitor job-related injuries and illnesses in the workplace.

7. *Recycling.* Most states require recycling of paper and aluminum, but in the near future, most states will also require recycling of fluorescent lightbulbs and ballasts, as well as plastic hangers.

8. *Dry cleaners.* Any dry cleaning establishment on site must provide the owner of the property with certification that it is in compliance with all EPA and OSHA rules and guideines.

9. *Underground storage tanks.* They must be identified to the

Environmental Protection Agency and maintained in accordance with applicable requirements.

10. *Hazard Communication Standard (HAZCOM).* The goal of HAZCOM is to ensure that employers and employees know the specific hazards associated with hazardous substances and how to work safely with them.

SECURING THE FUTURE

M aintenance in the shopping industry is more than just repairing equipment, fixing roof leaks and checking broken tiles. It is about securing the future of the asset, the shopping center, through a planned maintenance program. It is a proactive process rather than a reactive one and is aimed at changing operations in a structured manner in order to achieve superior performance.

Glossary

The glossary that follows is a listing of key definitions compiled from this outline, with several terms not defined in the outline added for your information. The terms are defined within the context of this shopping center management topic.

Adjustment billing   Reconciliation of budget estimates to actual expenses, resulting in either a credit or bill following year-end.

Administration fee   The cost of actually administering the common area of a shopping center; a standard addition to the overall cost of common-area maintenance (CAM), typically set at 15 percent of tenant CAM contribution but may vary due to negotiation between landlord and tenant.

Aggregate   Gravel, crushed stone, slag or marble embedded in flood coast of hot bitumen as top surface for built-up roofs.

Asbestos   Asbestos is a natural mineral that was processed into a fibrous substance and was widely used as a fire-retarding and insulation material. Its use has been mostly discontinued because some forms of the processed material have been found to be harmful to humans when exposed to the lungs. Asbestos fibers were added to floor tiles, roofing material, insulation on piping and other applications during construction. There are very definitive and sometimes expensive prescribed methods for removal and disposal of this material.

Asbestos abatement   A phased program to remove all asbestos-containing materials from the center. This is of particular concern where there is planned demolition and/or renovation of a portion of a shopping center in which asbestos and asbestos-containing materials (ACMs) might be disturbed. Asbestos-in-place insurance coverage is available as coverage for bodily injury, property damage, and third-party business interruption.

As-built plans   The final blueprints used by an architect when constructing a shopping center or a particular leased space within a center. As-builts contain the most up-to-date information about building conditions.

Asphalt emulsion   A method of sealer used to coat an asphalt parking lot. The emulsion is usually a diluted mixture of water, mineral filler, ash and rubber added to a coal tar or asphalt sealer.

Base sheet   A heavy sheet of felt, asbestos or organic material, often used as first ply in built-up roofing. Often saturated and factory coated with asphalt. Also used for roof insulation underlayment.

Bitumen   The generic term for a semisolid mixture of hydrocarbons derived from petroleum or coal; used to waterproof roofs. The two basic bitumens used in roofing are asphalt and coal tar pitch. Bitumens are the by-products of the oil-to-gasoline production process.

British thermal unit (BTU)   A BTU is the amount of heat required to raise the temperature of one pound of water at its maximum density [which occurs at a temperature of 39.1 degrees Fahrenheit (°F)] by one degree Fahrenheit.

Built-up roof (BUR)   A roofing membrane made of alternating layers or plies of felt adhered and made waterproof by the application of asphalt or coal tar bitumens.

Capital expenses   Major expenses that are typically amortized over time because it improves the asset. They usually include replacement of a storm sewer system, major HVAC equipment, roof and parking lot replacement, and major repairs that substantially improve the property over the original condition. Depending on the lease, most capital expenses are the responsibility of the landlord. Tenant improvement allowances are also considered capital expenses.

Chlorofluorocarbons (CFCs)   An ozone-depleting compound utilized by some HVAC units manufactured before 1995. The (U.S.) Federal Clean Air Act provides among other things that as of 1995 manufacturers of air conditioners and other appliances are prohibited from producing equipment that emits ozone-deleting compounds.

Closed circuit television (CCTV)   In shopping centers and other businesses this technology is sometimes used to supplement an on-site security staff or cover an area not staffed via off-site monitoring and notification of local law enforcement. Using CCTV places additional responsibility on the center staff to ensure that the equipment is properly installed, monitored, and maintained and that activity observed is responded to in a timely manner. Failure to perform any of these tasks may result in substantial liability.

Coal tar   One of two types of bitumen used to construct built-up roofs, derived from coking of coal. Used as waterproofing material for minimally sloped built-up roofs.

Common area maintenance (CAM)   Fee charged to tenants by the landlord for the maintenance of the common area of a center and specified in the lease agreement. Items charged to common area maintenance may include cleaning services, electricity, parking lot sweeping and maintenance, snow removal, security, and upkeep.

Compaction   The squeezing of a layer of asphalt by the addition of another asphalt layer or lift. Dense asphalt is usually required for parking lots and roadways.

Compressor   The workhorse of an HVAC (heating, ventilation, and air-conditioning) unit. The compressor is the hardware that "pushes" hot or cold air out of the system and into the center space. It acts as a refrigeration pump that circulates refrigerant and increases the pressure of refrigerant vapor.

Contractors   Prior to actual construction, the general contractor advises the owner, architect, and engineers on alternative methods of construction, prepares the project's construction budget and master schedule, and provides information and guidance on government approvals, safety requirements, bonding, insurance, local labor agreements, wages, and work rules. During the construction phase, the general contractor provides on-site organization and supervision for all elements of the work, provides cost statements and progress billings, and exercises overall financial and administrative control of the project.

Laborers who are hired by center managers for certain tasks are called contractors because the work is done according to a written agreement or contract. A landscape installation company, an HVAC repair company, and a company that provides security services are examples of contractors.

Core samples A testing process used to determine the condition of roofs or asphalt parking lots and roadways. A core is used to take a vertical sample of the roof or parking lot in question. An expert then surveys the layers to determine if the work was completed as agreed.

Cricket A roof slope or swell designed to run rainwater in a certain direction.

Curb stone A brace system designed to keep HVAC (heating, ventilation, and air-conditioning) units from touching a roof.

Delamination A built-up roof membrane failure due to separation of felt plies, often resulting in wrinkling or cracking.

Emergency procedures manual A manual given to tenants that gives important building information and safety procedures and also outlines procedures for various emergencies.

Fall Name of a measurement used for the installation of a drainage system in a parking lot. A fall is the slope or grade from one point, usually to a drain. Minimum required slope is 1 foot per 100 linear feet of parking lot.

Felt A fabric manufactured by interlocking fibers mechanically and with moisture and heat. Roofing felts are used to give membranes tensile strength and elasticity. They may be organic or inorganic compounds and are a vital component of built-up roof systems.

Fills Additional materials added to the substrate roof deck to alter its contour; for example, to achieve slope or to smooth out substrate.

Flashing Any protective and waterproofing material used to seal a junction of a roof and vertical wall rising above the roof, or a projection through a roof such as a chimney, vent pipe or skylight.

Flood coat A mopping of bitumen on exposed felts of a built-up roof to protect them from weather pending completion of the job.

Fluorescent light Type of lighting commonly found in a shopping center. Light is produced when current is passed through low-pressure mercury vapor inside a fluorescent-coated bulb.

Footcandle A measurement of light. The equivalent of illumination produced by a candle at the distance of one foot.

Grease interceptor Removes grease from waste water prior to entering municipal sewer systems. Grease is then removed from the interceptor.

Grease pans Metal reservoirs placed near ventilation units to catch grease before it touches the roof membrane.

Grease reclamation   Capturing grease from food operations and recycling or otherwise disposing of it to prevent entry into the sanitary or storm sewer system. Two systems are used for grease reclamation. The first is the standard grease trap and the second is an enzyme which, when placed into the drain systems, allows the grease to dissolve and flow through the drains.

Gross collectibles   The combination of all money transactions handled by the center management on behalf of the tenant. Taxes, minimum rent, percentage rent and CAM (common area maintenance) fall into this category. This figure is used to determine the management fee of the center.

Gross leasable area (GLA)   Normally the total area on which a shopping center tenant pays rent or can be leased. The GLA includes all selling space as well as storage and other miscellaneous space.

The square footage of a shopping center that can generate income by being leased to tenants. This figure does not include the area occupied by department stores or anchor tenants if these stores own their space instead of leasing space from the shopping center.

Gross lease   A lease in which the landlord pays 100% of all taxes, insurance and maintenance associated with the operation of a shopping center. The tenant pays a gross amount in which the landlord derrives gross revenues but does not receive separate recovery for extra charges.

Heat pump   A type of HVAC (heating, ventilation, air-conditioning) unit named for its internal mechanism, which runs on electricity.

Heating, ventilation and air-conditioning (HVAC) units
Fairly large equipment that handles all the heating, cooling and ventilation uses associated with a center.

Incandescent lighting   A lamp in which light is produced by electrically heating a filament. Used sparingly because of its cost inefficiencies.

Inspection   A detailed examination of the various physical assets of a shopping center.

Kettle   A vessel used to heat bitumen for roof application.

Lease   A contract transferring the right to the possession and enjoyment of property for a definite period of time for consideration, namely rent. The signed agreement between landlord and tenant that establishes rights and obligations for each party, sets standards and states what is recoverable from tenants for the maintenance process.

Leased space   The measurement used to define how much space a tenant has leased in a center. The leased premise is determined by measuring the distance between the middle walls of a space and the distance between front outside wall to back outside wall.

The total floor area designed for tenant occupancy and exclusive use, including basements, mezzanines, and upper floors. It is measured from the center line of joint partitions and from outside wall faces. In short, the leased premise is that area on which tenants pays rent; it is the area that produces income.

Lifts   The laying of a layer of asphalt on a prepared subgrade or another layer of asphalt.

Maintenance   The upkeep of the various physical assets and common area of a shopping center. Maintenance involves the preservation of what is already there. For example, patching the parking lot and relamping the lights; painting wall surfaces and replacing deteriorated caulking; rodding the sewer line and changing the oil in the vehicles; and in general doing those things that prolong the economic life of the property in its present forms.

Management fee   The fee charged by the fee manager or the owner to cover rental collection, administration, common area, maintenance, and tenant relations activities. Typically, a responsibility of an owner to a management company, the management fee is calculated from a negotiated percentage of the gross collectible of a shopping center. The fee usually includes the CAM (common area maintenance) charge.

The fee, whether a flat fee or a percentage of gross receipts, charged to the center owner for management services provided by the management company. This term is not to be confused with administrative fee, which is typically a tenant charge for administrating the common area.

Merchant criteria manual   Detailed description of construction or maintenance standards that merchants are required to observe. Also referred to as the Tenant Criteria Manual.

Merchant operating manual   A manual that describes how the retailer is expected to operate within the property. Areas covered include operating hours, trash removal requirements, parking area requirements, and general relationships and procedures the merchant is expected to follow and explain to their employees.

Modified bitumen   A type of built-up roof. Basically, a modified bitumen membrane consists of a combination of roofing felts and bitumen that has been modified by the addition of synthetic rubber or plastic compounds.

Offset   A reduction in the cost of percentage rent when a tenant meets a prearranged goal in another area, usually sales.

A deduction of specified expenses or investments from all or a portion of percentage rent.

Operating budget   An outline of how much income a shopping center has and how that income will be spent.

Includes all income other than sale of capital assets, offset by all items of expense other than depreciation and interest on debt and payments on debt principal or added investment.

Outparcels   Unused portions of a shopping center's site that constitute the perimeter areas, not including the center facility or parking lot, and that may be used or developed for similar or nonsimilar purposes.

Pad   The exact parcel of land on which a freestanding store stands or which may be developed for such a purpose.

Parking ratio   The relationship of space used for parking and necessary vehicular and pedestrian movement to gross leasable (or gross retail) area covered by buildings or space within the buildings. This relationship can be expressed in the number of car spaces per 1,000 square feet of leaseable areas.

Pass-through expenses   A tenant's portion of expense composed of common area maintenance, taxes and insurance, and any other expenses determined by the landlord to be paid by the tenant.

Patching   A procedure used in both roof and asphalt repair. In both cases, it involves repairing a tear, hole or other type of defect by filling with an appropriate compound.

Percentage rent   A percentage of the tenant's sales paid as rent. If additional percentage rent is paid after a predetermined sales level has been achieved, it is considered overage rent. The percentage factor is then applied to all sales over the present level (breakpoint). The payment by a tenant as rent of a specified percentage of the gross income from sales made upon the premises. Developers in shopping centers customarily charge a minimum rent plus a percentage rent (known as overage rent) when sales exceed a certain threshhold.

Perimeter protection   Devices designed to protect the exterior openings of a shopping center; for example, door locks and window bars.

Plies   A name for the layers of felts and bitumen formed during the creation of a built-up roof.

Ponding   Water that lies undrained on a roof or in parking lots over an extended period of time, which is likely to cause damage to the underlying area.

Preventive maintenance   Scheduled maintenance and repairs designed to enhance performance and extend the life of an asset.

Radon gas   A colorless, odorless gas produced naturally in certain areas of the world that rises from below the floor surface. It can accumulate in enclosed areas and be extremely harmful. Different state and province laws impose different requirements on landowners with regard to radon.

REA Reciprocal easement agreements between a shopping center and various anchors regarding how a given property is to be developed and maintained.

Recoating Procedure in both roof and parking lot maintenance in which a deteriorated surface is rejuvenated by a coat of, usually, a petroleum-based product.

Re-covering The placing of a new roof over an existing roof. This procedure may be done one time without the tearing-off of an existing roof membrane. Local codes will dictate reroofing policies.

Recovery rate Tenant reimbursement of CAM expenses/ total CAM expenses. Percentage rate may be below 100% if landlord has offered concessions or offset in order to attract or lease to a particular tenant. Percentage recovery rate may exceed 100% when administrative fees are added to CAM costs for tenant billing.

Replacement In a strict sense, it implies removing some portion of the property and restoring the missing part on a like-for-like basis.

Return on investment (ROI) analysis Formula used to determine the relative worth of a shopping center asset. There are many different kinds of analyses; they're usually used to determine if an asset should be repaired or replaced.

Roof deck   The prepared subsurface of a roof on which a membrane is laid.

Roof flashing   Metal band where roof and parapet meet. Prevents water seepage between joints.

Scupper   A hole in a parapet wall of a roof that allows water to flow into the roof drain. A scupper also acts as an overflow precaution in case of a gutter blockage.

Sealers   Liquid coatings used to protect asphalt parking lots and roadways.

Single ply   A type of roof made from a single layer of specially reinforced rubber or plastic.

Sleepers   Part of a bracing system that keeps HVAC (heating, ventilation, and air-conditioning) units anchored and off the roof and limits vibrations to the premises.

Slip and fall litigation   Name for the type of lawsuit brought against a shopping center when a consumer is hurt by slipping on a floor surface.

Slurry   A type of asphalt sealer. There are different types, and usage depends on the kind of roadway and desired protection.

Sodium light   A lamp in which light is produced by an electrical current passed through sodium vapor. Available in both high- and low-pressure applications.

Standard inspection   A daily, weekly or monthly examination of mechanical systems or other shopping center assets.

Standard operating procedure   Course of action that states precisely how a particular system of maintenance policy is to be conducted.

Standard Operating Procedures Manual   Booklet that outlines the center's maintenance policy.

Subgrade   The prepared surface on which asphalt is laid.

Tear-off   A roofing and asphalt procedure in which an old membrane or surface is removed as a prelude to replacement with a new product.

Tenant improvements   Building improvements that enhance a tenant's space. May be paid for by either landlord or tenant. In some cases, landlords provide an allowance for tenant improvements to induce the leasing of space. This is known as a tenant improvement (TI) allowance.

Tonnage   A measurement that determines the strength of an HVAC (heating, ventilation, and air-conditioning) system. Also used as a determinant to gauge air requirements for a tenant space. One ton of air is equivalent to 12,000 BTUs.

Trade fixture   An item specific to a tenant's business, usually not attached to the walls or floor; usually removed at lease expiration.

Triple net lease   Lease in which 100% of all taxes, insurance and maintenance associated with a shopping center is paid by the tenant.

Underground storage tanks (USTs)   Tanks used to house materials considered hazardous. In shopping centers, USTs typically contain petroleum-based products. They are subject to strict regulation with regard to testing, inspection, and replacement. Most states have established regulations for registering storage tanks and requirements for remediation of spills.

Volatile organic materials   Organic chemicals which are airborne contaminants and can be found in carpets, cleaning supplies, and even building materials and are strictly regulated by state laws.

Welcome book   Pamphlet given to tenants after signing a lease; it explains the ownership philosophy and introduces them to the center.